for my
children

A Mother's Journal
of Memories, Wishes
and Wisdom

Dionna Ford

 Ulysses Press

Published in the United States by
ULYSSES PRESS
P.O. Box 3440
Berkeley, CA 94703
www.ulyssespress.com

ISBN13: 978-1-61243-061-4
Library of Congress Catalog Number: 2012934451

Printed in the United States by Bang Printing

10 9 8 7 6 5 4 3 2 1

Acquisitions: Kelly Reed
Managing Editor: Claire Chun
Proofreader: Lauren Harrison
Design and layout: what!design @ whatweb.com
Illustrations: Melanie Mikecz

Distributed by Publishers Group West

Contents

Introduction

My mother has always been one of the first people I call for just about anything—to share a story, to ask for advice, to cry over a loss. Becoming a mama myself has made me see my mother in an entirely new light: She is not only nurturer and friend; she is also a woman with a whole lifetime of experiences and dreams I've never heard about.

But my mom and I rarely find the time (or make a concerted effort) to delve into family history or chat about fun, random questions. It seems that circumstance or distance always gets in the way, and I'm certain that our situation is not unique. *For My Children: A Mother's Journal of Memories, Wishes, and Wisdom* provides a way to chronicle a mother's history, to reveal stories and trivia that might otherwise be forgotten, to pass on generational wisdom, and most of all, to strengthen and create connections that may go untended. It is my hope that these writing prompts can be a catalyst for your own new discoveries and reconnections.

Motherhood

List the ways you feel closer or relate more to your mother now that you have children of your own:

What is some of the craziest parenting advice you ever received?

From lullabies to first recitals, music can narrate our lives in a way words never could. What songs and music have been important to you as a mother?

What can you remember as the highlights (and lowlights) from your pregnancy?

What do you remember changed most for you after first becoming a mother?

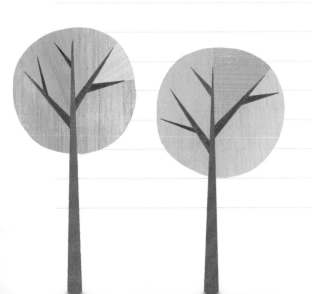

motherhood

List your wishes or prayers for your children:

What would you have changed about
your journey as a mother so far?

What do you miss the most about having your children living with you (or if you still have children at home, what will you miss the most)?

What sacrifices have you made to be the mother you are today?

What have been your favorite parts of being a mother?

What are your favorite gifts to give new mothers?

generosity

What are the moments that mothers
should be sure not to miss?

What activities and freedoms do you enjoy now that you have no children at home (or what are you looking forward to after your children are out on their own)?

What do you wish you had known as a new mother?

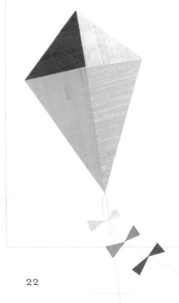

List some of the strangest things you have ever done as a parent:

What experiences helped you become more confident as a mother?

What do you most enjoy (or look forward to) sharing with your children now that they are adults that you could not when they were younger?

nurture

List interesting (and little-known) facts about your children—something that might even surprise them:

You know you're a mom when:

Crayon on the wall. A new haircut—by the four year old. A dozen eggs broken on the kitchen floor because your toddler attempted to make you pancakes. What are some of the most memorable scenes you have walked into as a mother?

List some of the things you have learned
from your children:

play

What are some of your favorite memories of your child from birth to five years of age?

What are some of your favorite memories of your child from six to twelve years of age?

What are some of your favorite memories of your child's teenage years?

It is hard to watch our children in pain, unsure of themselves, or going through rough times. What have been the hardest things you have had to watch your child live through?

How do you measure success as a mother?

Family and Home

Whether it's a lively annual reunion, a crazy Aunt Sally, or embarrassing family Halloween costumes, every family has its oddities and quirks. What are some of your family's quirks?

What wisdom have you learned from past generations of your family?

Of all our five senses, our sense of smell has the strongest link to memory. What smells do you associate with your family—with home?

What family traditions do you remember from
your own childhood?

What are your favorite family celebrations or traditions from your family, and how did they get started?

What are some of your most beloved family treasures, and where did they come from?

What have you learned from your in-laws that have made you a better in-law (or would make someone be a better in-law)?

celebration

Birthday cakes—they can either be wild successes or amusing wrecks. What are some of the most memorable cakes you've made or been served?

How has being a mother changed your relationship as a partner?

List some of your family's favorite
recreational activities:

What are (or were) your favorite family recipes?

List some interesting facts about your extended family members (including some your children might not know):

If you had to compare your family members to fictional characters (from books, movies, etc.), who would they be?

Children

The world looks different for each new generation. What changes stood out to you between the time you were a child and the time your children were growing up?

Remember that time you wouldn't let your child do what all of his friends were doing? Surely the same thing happened when you were a child—what do you remember arguing about with your parents?

individuality

List some of the ways you saw your child
becoming more independent:

What kind of fads were all the rage when you were young—and which ones do you wish had never fallen out of fashion?

What other names did you consider for your children?

In what ways are your children like you?

In what ways are your children different
from you?

What do you value most about
your children?

If an adult's life is all about work, a child's life is all about play. What games did your children love to play—and which ones did you like to join them in?

What people—friends, family, teachers—
were important to you as a child?

What experiences do you feel are
important for children to have?

What moments have made you most proud of your child?

What mementos have you kept from the time when your children were growing up?

nostalgia

What special things have you done for your children to create lifetime memories?

If you could ask your parents
anything, what would you ask?

Life Wisdom
and Wishes

List the places in the world you would like
to travel to and why:

adventure

On counting blessings: What have you been most grateful for in life?

What events—both big and small—have shaped your definition of the meaning of life?

What have been some of your most embarrassing moments, and how did you react?

We all want to simplify our lives—what tips and tricks can you offer to make life simpler?

If you had unlimited funds, what would you do with the money?

What have you been putting off until
"someday" that you wish you hadn't?

You know those moments that take your breath
away? What were yours?

What fears have you conquered?

hope

Your keys to happiness are:

What have been the most difficult
decisions of your life to make?

What are ten experiences every adult should have?

If life had a rewind button, what moments would you want to relive?

Do you like surprises? What have been some of your favorite—and least favorite—surprises in life?

What lasting impressions or impact would you like to leave on the world?

strength

What inspires you?

In what ways do you live life to the fullest?

The best things come to those who wait. What were the best things in your life that you had to wait for?

Take a walk today. List the most interesting things you saw:

How have you learned to handle life when
you felt discouraged?

determination

Bravery can mean many different things—what are the bravest acts you have witnessed?

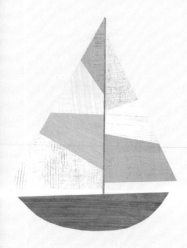

What have proved to be some of the most difficult times in your life to tell the truth?

List the best ways to beat boredom:

List the many wonderful things you've discovered about growing older:

In what ways have you had to stand up for yourself or others?

How have you pursued happiness?

Sometimes it's nice to have a "plan B." What are helpful ways to remain flexible in the face of changed plans?

Easy ways to show compassion to your fellow humans:

Life is short. Don't waste it _____
(fill in the blank with things not worth wasting
time, energy, and life on).

Wear clean underwear. Go with your gut. Seize the day. What are some of the most useful life lessons you can pass on to your children?

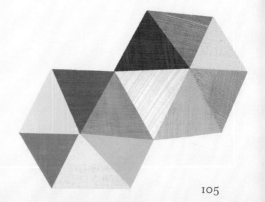

Don't sweat the small stuff. What small stuff have you sweated that you wish you hadn't? What small stuff were you able to let go of?

What lifts your spirits when you experience sadness or depression?

What quotes, poems, or scripture have been inspirational to you?

The best things in life are free.
*What freebies have made your life
fuller?*

Holidays that *should* be invented:

What is the best advice you have ever
received?

Is there anything you wish you'd said to someone—your mom, your child, your partner—but you never did?

Who have you considered to be your closest friends—from childhood onward—and where are they now?

Love and

Relationships

What made you fall for the love of your life?

cherish

Mom the Love Counselor: What tips would you offer to couples for maintaining a healthy, happy relationship?

What do you wish you had discussed with your partner before you married? (Alternatively, what do you believe couples should discuss before marrying?)

Some people show their love by giving gifts, others by expressing themselves using words or touch. How do you like to express your love? What are some of the most loving things you have done for others?

Have you ever nursed a broken heart? What did you find were the best ways to heal the hurt?

What do you wish you had known as a new wife/partner?

comfort

What are effective ways to let go of anger or hatred?

What activities do you and your partner enjoy as a couple?

Ten great questions to spark conversation on a first date:

You in the World

Many people remember where they were or what they were doing when major world events happened. Of the world events that had an impact on you, can you recall where you were when they occurred?

Kids don't vote, but moms do—what issues were important to you as a mother?

Oh, the places you'll go. From the trips you took as a child with your own family, to your honeymoon and all of the vacations that followed, where have you traveled and which locations were your favorites?

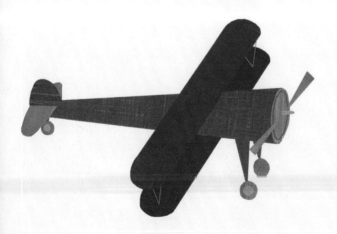

What people or events have most shaped your spirituality?

journey

If you could change the world, what would you do?

What culturally or socially historic events
have you witnessed, and how did they
change your worldview?

List the ways your faith, religion, or beliefs have influenced your life:

What do you do (or wish you would do regularly) to take care of your health?

Who makes you laugh, and what do you laugh about?

Are there any jobs or career paths you wish you'd pursued?

On Being You

wisdom

A massage … conversation over a pot of tea … unexpected notes in the mail … What have friends and family done for you over the years that have made you smile and feel loved?

Who have been your role models and mentors, and why were these people important to you?

What are your passions in life, and what have you done to pursue them?

What could your friends and family do for you now to make life easier or more enjoyable?

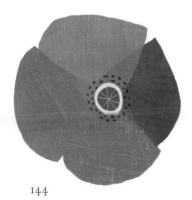

Without balance, we cannot be effective or compassionate mothers, lovers, friends, or women. How have you found balance? What activities do you turn to when you feel out of balance?

What books have you worn out the covers on?

Everyone has an indulgence—what are yours?

People would be surprised if they knew you:

What kinds of things have you been recognized for (awards, etc.)?

List some of your favorite things that you have made (crafts, recipes, etc.):

talent

What are your go-to recipes for social events?

What are the themes of your recurring,
favorite, or worst dreams?

Do you have any phobias? If so, do you remember where they came from?

Make your own list! Everything must center around this topic: "Firsts."

Make your own list! Everything must center around this topic: "Favorites."

Some of us collect things, others collect people, a few of us collect worries. What collections have you made?

What are your favorite ways to express yourself creatively?

What mementos have you kept from your own life over the years?